What's the Place Value?

Shirley Duke

Rourke
Educationa
rourkeeducational

Teacher Notes available at
rem4teachers.com

www.rourkeeducationalmedia.com

PHOTO CREDITS: Cover: © Bowie15, adlifemarketing; Title Page, Page 4-8, 10,12-14,16-18, 21: © Jill Fromer

Edited by Precious McKenzie

Cover design by Teri Intzegian
Interior design by Renee Brady

Library of Congress PCN Data

What's the Place Value? / Shirley Duke
(Little World Math)
ISBN 978-1-61810-075-7 (hard cover)(alk. paper)
ISBN 978-1-61810-208-9 (soft cover)
Library of Congress Control Number: 2011944385

Rourke Educational Media
Printed in the United States of America,
North Mankato, Minnesota

rourkeeducationalmedia.com

customerservice@rourkeeducationalmedia.com • PO Box 643328 Vero Beach, Florida 32964

One's place. Ten's place. What do they mean?

ten's place	one's place
?	?

Count with me.

1 2 3 4 5 6 7 8 9

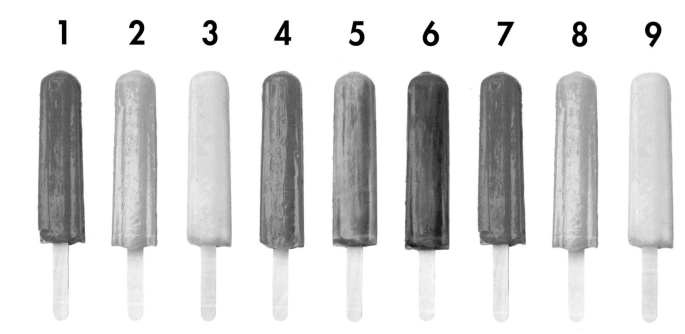

Numbers show how many.

ten's place	9
?	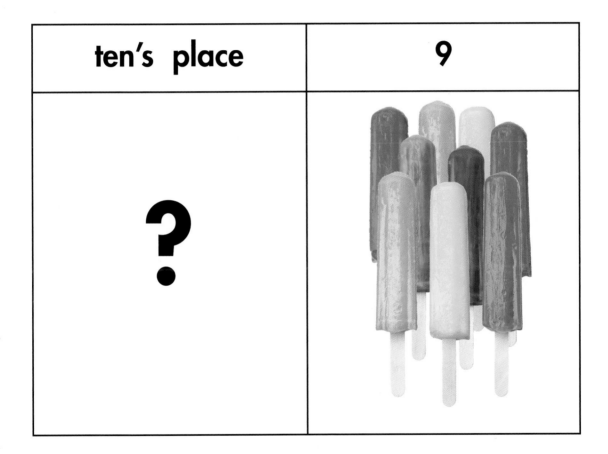

Add one more.

1 2 3 4 5 6 7 8 9 10

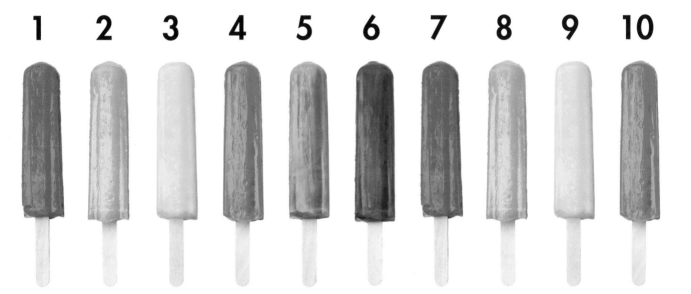

We have a group of ten!

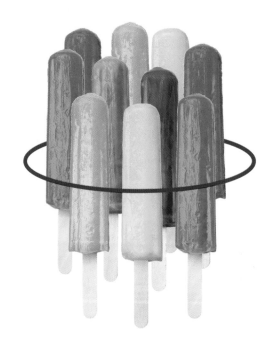

Ten needs a place.

Where do we put one set of ten?

ten's place	one's place

It belongs in the ten's place!

ten's place	one's place

Do you know that zero equals no ones?

ten's place	one's place
1	0

Now add four more.

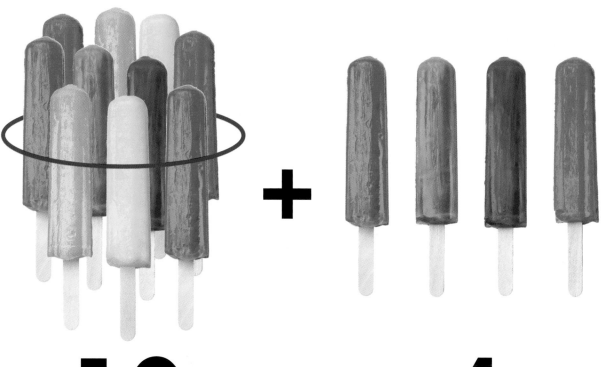

10 + **4**

What's the place value?

1 set of ten.

4 ones.

ten's place	one's place
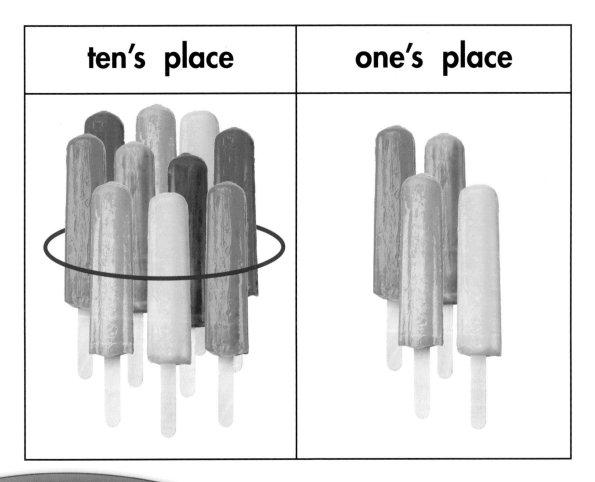	

What does that equal?
14 popsicles for 14 friends!

1 set of tens plus 4 ones =

14

Now, add ten more.

ten's place	one's place
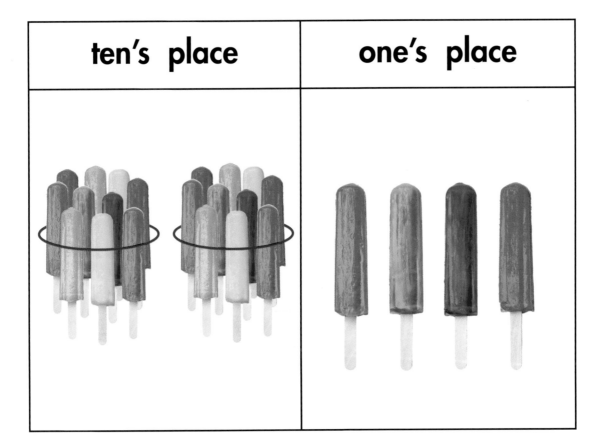	

What's the place value?

2 sets of ten.

4 ones.

ten's place	one's place
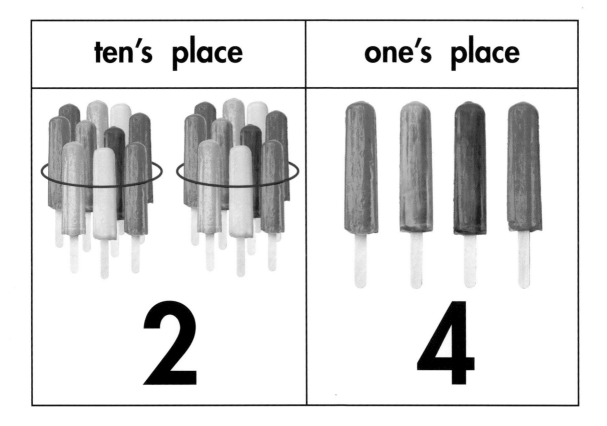	
2	**4**

2 sets of tens + 4 ones = 24

4 sets of tens + 2 ones = 42

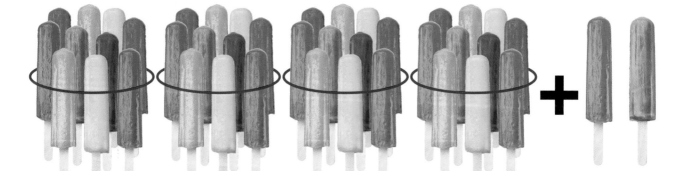

Which is more?

ten's place	one's place
2	**4**

ten's place	one's place
4	**2**

Which is more?

$$3 \text{ tens } + 5 \text{ ones } = 35$$

$$5 \text{ tens } + 3 \text{ ones } = 53$$

53!

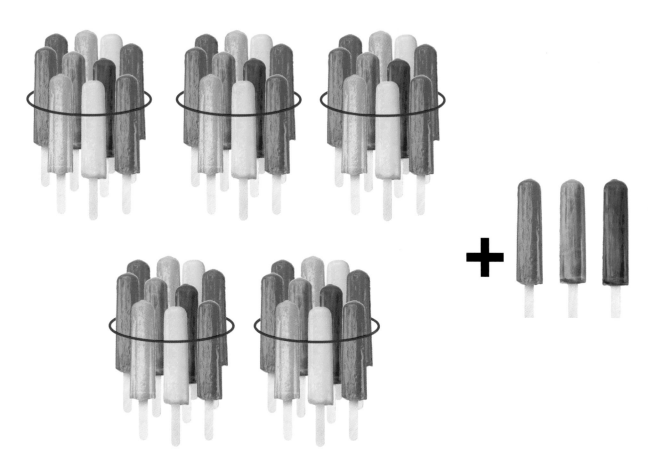

What's the place value of 53?

How many tens?

ten's place	one's place
5	

How many ones?

ten's place	one's place
	3

Five sets of tens. Three ones.
50 + 3 = 53. Place value matters!

ten's place	one's place
5	3

Index

Websites

www.learningbox.com/Base10/BaseTen.html

www.linkslearning.org/Kids/1_Math/2_Illustrated_Lessons/ 3_Place_Value/

www.superteacherworksheets.com/place-value/placeval-tensones.pdf

About the Author

Shirley Duke has done math all her life. This is her first time writing a math book. She wrote about place value from her place in Texas.

Ask The Author!
www.rem4students.com